EXTREME SPORTS

Pointers for Pushing the Limits

PREPARING FOR GAME DAY

PREPARING FOR GAME DAY

EXTREME SPORTS
Pointers for Pushing the Limits

Peter Douglas

MASON CREST

Mason Crest
450 Parkway Drive, Suite D
Broomall, Pennsylvania 19008
(866) MCP-BOOK (toll free)

First printing
9 8 7 6 5 4 3 2 1

ISBN (hardback) 978-1-4222-3916-2
ISBN (series) 978-1-4222-3912-4
ISBN (ebook) 978-1-4222-7871-0

Cataloging-in-Publication Data on file with the Library of Congress

QR CODES AND LINKS TO THIRD-PARTY CONTENT

CONTENTS

KEY ICONS TO LOOK FOR:

Words to understand: These words with their easy-to-understand definitions will increase the reader's understanding of the text while building vocabulary skills.

Sidebars: This boxed material within the main text allows readers to build knowledge, gain insights, explore possibilities, and broaden their perspectives by weaving together additional information to provide realistic and holistic perspectives.

Educational Videos: Readers can view videos by scanning our QR codes, providing them with additional educational content to supplement the text. Examples include news coverage, moments in history, speeches, iconic sports moments and much more!

Text-dependent questions: These questions send the reader back to the text for more careful attention to the evidence presented there.

Research projects: Readers are pointed toward areas of further inquiry connected to each chapter. Suggestions are provided for projects that encourage deeper research and analysis.

Series glossary of key terms: This back-of-the book glossary contains terminology used throughout this series. Words found here increase the reader's ability to read and comprehend higher-level books and articles in this field.

 ## WORDS TO UNDERSTAND:

affirmation: a statement of the existence or truth of something

imagery: the formation of mental images, figures, or likenesses of things or of such images collectively

spirulina: blue-green algae of the genus *Spirulina*, sometimes added to food for its nutrient value.

Chapter 1

COMPETITION DAY

Extreme sports, or action sports as they are also commonly called, is a term that refers to a wide variety of activities. The spectrum is so broad that the physical requirements can be quite different for athletes from one discipline to another. A rock climber and a powerboat racer will have very different sets of skills. In general, however, when competition time approaches, these competitors are all athletes who need to be prepared to perform at a high level.

Skateboarding is perhaps the one activity that epitomizes the slacker mentality of extreme sports. Old-school skateboarders had a reputation for eating a lot of junk food and partying into the wee hours of the night, treating their bodies in ways that athletes in training would not normally do.

When it first started in the 1970s, skateboarding was more of a lifestyle than a sport, and those who did it did not consider themselves to be athletes.

" Do it (skateboarding) every day. When you do something every single day and you get really good at it, you'll keep progressing to the level you want to get to. "

In this century, however, skateboarding and many other action sports are big-time, big-money enterprises, and the competitors have evolved to take it all much more seriously. There is still some of that counterculture attitude, but when it comes to

– Greg Lutzka, three-time X Games skateboard street medalist

Ultramarathon runners, like this 2016 competitor in a forty-five-mile (seventy-two-kilometer) event in the Canary Islands, fuel with carbs on race day

"You always want to have your knees bent a little bit no matter what you're doing. When you're straight legging, you put yourself in a great amount of danger, especially when you're on the ramps."

– Brian Aragon, aggressive inline skating legend

performing, the athletes know they have to have to have an athlete's approach.

SMART START

On competition days, it is important to get the body off to the right start to set up the rest of the day. That means choosing the right food for that all-important first meal. Different types of athletes choose different sources of fuel. Here are a few examples.

Ultra runners (distance runners who run anywhere from thirty- to one hundred-mile [fifty- to one hundred sixty-kilometer] races) are looking to fuel up with carbs while also including some protein. A breakfast of Greek yogurt, cereal, a banana, and some chocolate milk would provide the necessary balance. On days with late start times, about two hours before the race, a bowl of olive oil fried rice with pineapple, spinach, and two eggs tops up the energy reserves.

Climbers might take a different approach to nutrition on the day of a climb. They are looking for major sources of protein. To keep the body strong for those long days on the rock face, a good start might be a four-egg omelet with chopped arugula and carrots.

For surfers, they are looking for a good energy boost right before they charge the waves. Avoiding refined sugar and other processed foods as energy sources is a smart move. Instead, many surfers like a power-packed smoothie about an hour before getting on their boards. Low-fat yogurt blended with protein powder, goji berries, a banana, bee pollen, spinach, assorted raw nuts or seeds, coconut water, flaxseed oil, **spirulina**, and maca will help keep a surfer close to the curl all day.

Big mountain skiing requires a good dose of courage and a balance of carbs and protein to get down the most challenging runs. The day starts with a protein-based breakfast, such as an almond milk smoothie with berries, pine pollen, plain kefir, and nuts. Then, about an hour before heading up the mountain, it is time for some carbs. A cup of fried rice with broccoli and an egg mixed in does the trick.

BE FLEXIBLE

Radical maneuvers are hard to pull off, and they are hard on the body as well. Long gone are the days of grabbing the board and sprinting into the sea or strapping on the snowboard and dropping straight into the halfpipe. Today's action sport athletes realize that if they want to spend their time perfecting routines and nailing tough tricks rather than rehabbing injuries, they need to get the body and its muscles ready to compete.

Here are some examples of effective pre-competition stretches used by action sports athletes from J. Taylor at DrftingThru.com:

"Understand that surfing, like life, is going to be difficult. You're not going to get instant gratification. You're going to have to work at it to get good at it. The harder you work at it the more fun ultimately you're going to have."

– Shaun Tomson, 1977 International Professional Surfers world champion

One of the biggest keys to surfing is that you have to be a great paddler and learn how to catch the waves and how to read the waves. The best way to do that is just to put time in the water.

– Corey Lopez, three-time X Games gold medalist

"Snowboards are made for powder. They love floating on top. So just give a little lean with your back foot, make sure you keep your speed up, and keep your weight on your back foot to keep the nose up."

– Erin Simmons, Olympian and X Games medalist

"Step one to a backflip, you're going to want to know the speed so you don't go too big or too small. As you're coming to the jump you're going to want to be very flat based, no carve or anything, because you can catch your edge."
– Jaeger Bailey,
YouTube snowboarding sensation

CROSSED-LEG GLUTE STRETCH

Lie on your back, and bend your legs so that your feet are flat on the floor. Bring your right foot up, and cross it over your left leg so that your right ankle rests just below your left knee. Put your hands around your upper left leg, and lift it up toward your chest. Feel the stretch on your right leg and slowly pull closer until you reach your limit. Hold this stretch for 30 seconds, and then repeat with your left leg.

TWISTING OBLIQUE STRETCH

Sit down with your legs stretched out in front of you, straight and side by side, with toes pointing to the sky. Twist at your hips to the right, keeping your back straight, but move through your shoulders, and bring your head around so that you look directly to your right. Bring your arms around at the same time, and place your fingertips on the ground to your right-hand side. Hold this position for thirty seconds, then repeat on your left side.

SIMPLE AB STRETCH

Get onto your belly, and lie flat and straight with your arms by your sides. Bring your arms up into the press-up position, and push up, lifting your upper body up at the same time. Your hips should stay flat on the floor but be pushing into the ground. Arch your back, and look up toward the sky. You should feel your stomach and abdominal muscles stretch out; hold this position for thirty seconds, and then relax.

OVERHEAD TRICEP STRETCH

Stand in a relaxed position, and lift up your right arm straight, with your fingers pointing to the sky. Bend your arm at the elbow to bring your hand down behind you, resting on your back between your shoulder blades. Use your left hand to hold and pull down on your right elbow, and hold this stretch for thirty seconds. Rest a moment, then repeat with your left arm.

BACKHAND BICEP STRETCH

From a standing position, bring both your hands behind your back, and clasp your hands together. Let your shoulders drop, and push your arms out away from your back, lifting your hands up toward the sky. Reach your limit, and hold your arms in this position for thirty seconds.

LIE-DOWN LOWER BACK STRETCH

Lay flat on the floor looking toward the sky—body, legs, and arms straight. Lift your knees up, and bring them to your chest with your legs bent and tucked in. Lift your arms up, and link your hands over your shins at the same time. Hold for thirty seconds, then return to your original position slowly and in control.

A long-distance swimmer stretches out his triceps before taking to the water.

BENDING BODY AND NECK STRETCH

Stand up straight with your legs slightly apart in line with your hips. Take a deep breath, then as you exhale lean forward, and lower your head to the ground. Bend at the hips as far as you'll go, bringing your upper body close to your legs (keep your legs straight), and move your arms around your legs to hold you in position. Keep this position for thirty seconds, then relax, and stand up slowly, bending your knees if necessary.

LUNGING QUAD STRETCH

Get onto your knees with your shins on the floor. Lunge forward with your right leg so that your knee is bent at ninety degrees and your foot is placed flat on the ground. Your left leg should be stretched out behind you. Put your hand on your right knee, and push forward through your hips. You'll feel your right leg quad muscle stretch; hold this position for thirty seconds then repeat with the left leg.

> 66 Even on concrete you'll start with both feet down. Put them in front of your foot pegs. And the reason you start with both feet on the ground is because it balances out the bike perfectly. 99

– Ricky Carmichael, ten-time motocross national champion

A skyrunner stretches her hamstrings before a competition in Iceland.

STRAIGHTFORWARD HAMSTRING STRETCH

Lie on your back with your body straight. Lift your right leg up, and keep it straight; don't bend your knee. Use your hands to hold the back of your upper leg, and keep lifting your leg up so that your foot is pointed to the sky. Hold this stretch for thirty seconds, then repeat it with your left leg.

V-SHAPE THIGH AND GROIN STRETCH

Sit on the ground, and position your legs like a V out in front of you, the wider apart, the better, with your back straight and upright. Lean forward, pivoting at your hips, and hold your arms out as you bend as far forward as you can. Hold this for thirty seconds; the further you push forward, the more you'll feel it on the insides of your legs.

"You're going to come up the ramp, and you're not jumping up, you're jumping forward, but not nose down. You've got to be going fast enough to clear the jump, and as you take off the ramp, push through, forward off the ramp."

– Harry Main, pro BMX rider

Watch Danny Way get ready to jump the Great Wall of China on his skateboard.

WHAT DO YOU THINK?

You have done all the training, eaten effectively, and stretched to warm up your muscles. Now it is time to jump off that cliff, drop down that megaramp, or build speed for that 1080 in the halfpipe. How do extreme athletes psych themselves up to do the things they do? There a number of different techniques that athletes from different sports use.

Speed alpinist Ueli Steck of Switzerland uses autogenic training to prepare himself mentally for the task of climbing some of the world's toughest mountain faces faster than anyone else. Autogenic training is a German technique that is executed by repeating a series of visualizations to achieve a state of relaxation. Going through these visualizations before performing can help athletes channel their fear and get to a relaxed place in their minds.

Skateboard legend Danny Way uses reflection to help get him in the zone mentally when standing at the top of one of his megaramps. He takes some time to think of all the good things in his life. Then, he goes a step further, thinks about all of the mentors he has had in his long career,

> ❝ On jumps that I can barely get over on my 125, I'm hitting them in the correct gear, I'm back on the bike a little bit trying to compress that back end to get the bike to lift up the most. Right when that front end starts coming up, I'm lifting up at the bars, pulling it into my chest and pulling the bike up as far as I possibly can. ❞
>
> – Ryan Hughes, professional motocross driver

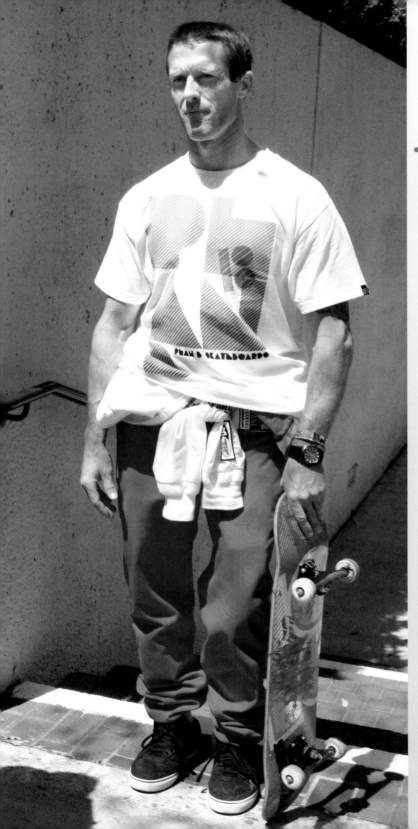

Skateboarding legend Danny Way sometimes uses reflection to prepare himself mentally before a big event.

15

> "When you're approaching a jump, you want to have your ankles flexed, your knees flexed and your hips flexed. Then as you approach, you're going to have a slight extension in your knees and you're going to come up, and that's going to give you the pop."
>
> *– James Webb,*
> *professional freestyle skier*

and recalls all the positive feedback he has received from each of them.

Whatever the technique, from autogenic training to reflection or **imagery** to **affirmation**, find one that works for you, and set aside some time immediately before it is time to compete to get yourself in a place mentally where you can be laser focused on the task at hand.

TEXT-DEPENDENT QUESTIONS:

1. Give an example of an ideal breakfast for a climber on the day of a big climb.

2. Name four examples of effective pre-competition stretches.

3. How do extreme athletes psych themselves up to do the things they do? Name a few techniques.

RESEARCH PROJECT:

Take some time, and put together a pregame routine for yourself. Be detailed in each element, outlining specific numbers of repetitions for drills, etc. Be sure to make the routine specific to your sport. Outline meals, rest, and all the necessary components that you feel could help best prepare you before a big competition.

WORDS TO UNDERSTAND:

adrenaline: a substance that is released in the body of a person who is feeling a strong emotion (such as excitement, fear, or anger) and that causes the heart to beat faster and gives the person more energy

expedition: a journey, especially by a group of people for a specific purpose (such as to explore a distant place or to do research)

hypothermia: a condition in which the temperature of the body is very low

Chapter

THE RIGHT MIND-SET

RISK ASSESSMENT AND SAFETY PLANNING

Participants in extreme sports need to assess the possible dangers ahead of time; this means they plan out all possible scenarios and think through all their consequences. Failure to do so can result in serious injuries or even have fatal consequences. Before embarking on any trips, several factors have to be considered:

- Check the weather conditions for the day.

- Wear clothing appropriate to the weather and the sport, including a helmet and protective padding.

- Determine any important aspects or obstacles of the natural terrain that might affect safety and performance.

- Make sure you have the necessary equipment stored appropriately. Is there any new equipment you need to purchase or any maintenance that needs to be done?

- Do you have necessary emergency equipment? First-aid kits and survival equipment are necessary parts of any extreme-sport **expedition** for heli-skiing, canyoning, etc. Also be sure to find out where the nearest hospitals will be to your location, and have emergency contacts standing by.

- Warm up and stretch before any intense activity.

Considering all of these types of measures ahead of time will allow you to participate worry free and focus on the activity at hand. Ask for expert advice, and make a checklist of the equipment needed in all kinds of situations. The guidance of an experienced instructor is crucial for ensuring safety.

Many extreme sports are dangerous, so it is particularly important that athletes be well prepared to compete.

MENTAL PREPARATION

Participants need to be mentally sharp and focused to perform well and stay safe in extreme sports. Through mental preparation, each performance can be kept more consistent as well. To do this, you need to always follow a mental routine prior to and during any activities. This is especially true in those sports that take you into challenging environments, like canyoning or mountaineering. This routine will include the following:

- Use complete concentration. When you're in the midst of the challenges of an extreme sport, you can't afford to let your thoughts wander outside the boundaries of the task at hand. Extreme sports are dangerous and should only be done with great concentration. So before you begin, shift your attention away from everyday life, and focus on what you are doing.

- Be strategic. Never venture out without a plan. Bring maps with highlighted routes, and plan the things that you want to do while on the trip. With a predetermined course, you can also let your friends and family know where you'll be, so they are able to locate you in an emergency.

- Be careful, but have confidence. Know your surroundings, and be sure you are familiar with your sport. After physical training and years of practice, understand that you are prepared. Remain positive and relaxed.

- Execute well. Don't expect any particular outcomes, but simply try your best. There is no gain in dwelling on what could happen. Stay in the moment.

- Practice. Always do a test run on the same or a similar path. Getting to know the course can bring familiarity and build confidence.

DON'T STRESS OUT

Be prepared that anything could happen. This doesn't mean you scare yourself by imagining the worst. Instead, you mentally picture the aspects that could go wrong and then calmly prepare a solution for each. People who do this are better able to face hazards when they encounter them in real life. Resolving any potential problems when you have plenty of time to think about them, when you aren't in any actual danger, allows you to fall back on these solutions automatically should you actually encounter that danger. The technique known as imagery can help with this type of preparation.

> It's like a switch that you've got to flip that kind of closes off everything around, and you put on your channel vision and say 'Alright, the only thing I'm going to think about and the only thing I'm going to do right now is walk up those stairs, put my board down, stand on it and jump that thing.'
>
> – Danny Way, five-time X Games gold medalist

The ocean, for example, can be a dangerous environment. Imagine you are surfing when you are suddenly caught in a powerful riptide and dragged out to sea. Picture this scenario as clearly as possible, including the sound of seagulls overhead, the heaving waves around you, and the salty taste of the water in your mouth. As you imagine that the water is relentlessly pulling your body, convince yourself to remain calm and confident. Then, using the advice of an experienced surfer, remember to swim diagonally toward the beachfront (because facing the beachfront directly only guarantees that the current will continue to hold you back until you are exhausted). If necessary, let the riptide carry you further out until its force disappears, and then swim back. Picture yourself swimming to shore, reaching solid ground safely.

Extreme sports involve precision maneuvers that require intense concentration.

Dangerous situations can be avoided and injuries may be prevented by rigorous mental preparation. In the event of an actual problem, people are usually too stressed to think properly on the spot, and therefore, prior planning can help save lives.

A famous American president once said, "The only thing we have to fear is fear itself." Fear in the face of stressful and unplanned situations during extreme sports is only natural, but the fear and stress themselves can be dangerous. As the human body feels the **adrenaline** rush during these moments, the trick is to channel the adrenaline toward a purposeful action to avoid injury. By thinking positively and logically, the mind can stay focused and avoid panic. The goal is to counter each negative thought with a positive one.

You will feel more confident if you carry yourself more confidently. In case of a problem, raise your head, and square your shoulders to face the issue as

Learning to control fear is an important component of being mentally prepared for extreme sports.

though you feel calm. Simply by pretending to be decisive and confident, the mind will start to mimic the body, and your mental focus will return.

Controlling your fear will help make participating in action sports safer and more fun. Instead of being consumed by fright and panic, individuals can mentally prepare themselves and their bodies to deal with any scenario.

Mountaineer and BASE jumper Joby Ogwyn talks about the mental toughness needed to climb Mount Everest.

We have all heard the expression that refers to someone who seems to seek out dangerous situations as being an "adrenaline junkie." The concept is that they are addicted to danger, but could a person actually be addicted to the body chemical that is adrenaline? The body releases adrenaline when put in situations that elicit fear, excitement, or anger. Can a person become dependent on the feelings he or she gets when the chemical is released, or is it the behavior that has the potential to be habit forming?

In the scientific community, there is no study that has concluded that these junkies are actual addicts. What studies do suggest is that dopamine, a brain chemical that evokes intense satisfaction after a challenging or difficult task has been accomplished, might be the real culprit. That feeling of satisfaction may be what these junkies really crave rather than the feeling of fear or danger.

There is also the theory that the addiction is more behavioral than chemical, like a gambling addiction. The compulsion is just as real as a chemical dependency and just as hard to overcome. Adrenaline junkies are in theory addicted to the action, the excitement, and the thrill of pushing boundaries and limits. In practice, however, few so-called adrenaline junkies fit the criteria for the definition of an addict. So the jury is still out on whether thrill seekers actually have some sort of dependency issue. All they know is they just can't get enough.

Helmets should be labeled by the U.S. CPSC, and athletes should also wear knee, elbow, and other appropriate pads as needed.

GEAR YOU NEED

Action sports can be dangerous, and most are more dangerous than traditional sports. Each action sport has its own unique identity and, therefore, its own safety equipment. You'll need to research the correct safety equipment for each sport and its uses. For most action sports, the most important safety equipment is a light fiberglass or impact helmet. When purchasing a helmet, you should try it on, adjust the fasteners, and shake your head; a good helmet should be comfortable and able to stay firmly in place without slipping. Additionally, helmets should be labeled by the U.S. Consumer Product Safety Commission (CPSC) to guarantee that the helmet has been tested and is up to par with standards. If a helmet has been damaged in an accident, throw it away, and buy a new one. Other important equipment for many extreme sports includes wrist guards, elbow pads, and kneepads. Velcro® on pads should be cleaned regularly to avoid lint buildup that might cause them to not hold firm.

To take up inline skating, for example, research finding a pair of comfortable and practical skates with strong ankle support. Stopping should be one of the first things you learn. Another way to minimize injury is to learn to fall with the least impact, such as a rolling fall. These procedures can help minimize common injuries to inline skaters, such as wrist sprains, fractures, and trauma to elbows, shoulders, and the head.

These techniques can often be applied broadly across the spectrum of action sports. For example, in skateboarding, learning to fall is absolutely essential in minimizing injury. Padding and a helmet are also crucial to safety. An added aspect of safety for skateboarding comes from specially designed skateboard shoes, which contain a rubber sole to avoid slippage. These can help avoid common skateboard injuries such as sprains, fractures, head trauma, cuts, and bruises.

CLIMATE-RELATED GEAR

Very few action sports take place indoors, so athletes will usually need gear that protects them from climate and weather.

WHEN IT'S COLD OUT THERE

Depending on the sport, frostbite and **hypothermia** are two of the main conditions possible in severe cold. Wearing several layers of clothing traps

In cold-weather conditions, athletes should wear appropriate clothing to protect from frostbite or hypothermia.

heat better than one thick layer of clothing. Layers of thermal clothing are recommended. Mountaineers and Arctic explorers sometimes wear up to five layers, including thermal underwear, an undershirt, a woolen sweater, a jacket, and a waterproof coat. Since the outer extremities (your hands and feet) have weaker blood circulation and higher heat loss, they tend to become frostbitten first.

Fabrics that are waterproof or that will not trap moisture are the most practical for cold-weather activities. Clothing made from this type of fabric minimizes the sweat that may be trapped inside the jacket, while water is kept out, allowing you to stay dry and comfortable outdoors.

Insulated, waterproof boots with soles that provide good traction are also necessary. Boots can also offer ankle support and heel padding, which lessen the stress on the joints and legs when hiking over rough terrain. Boot tread should provide the traction you need to keep from slipping on ice or snow. Finally, snow goggles with adequate UV protection are necessary for proper eye protection. When sunlight reflects off snow, it can cause snow blindness; goggles can prevent watery eyes, blurred vision, and painful eyes. In addition, goggles protect the eyes in the event of a fall.

WHEN IT'S HOT OUT THERE

Hot environments present a different but equally dangerous set of obstacles. People who participate in water sports usually wear few clothes, and sunburns account for most of the injuries. Without proper sunscreen applied every few hours, skin will burn. Higher SPF sunscreen can offer greater protection,

In hot-weather conditions, high SPF sunscreen should be worn, and athletes should be aware of the signs of heatstroke during periods of prolonged sun exposure.

Sports like body boarding are relatively low cost compared to others that require more equipment.

and waterproof sunscreen will protect skin in water. Sunburns are painful—and they can eventually lead to skin cancer. Outside of water, exposure to long periods of sun can cause heatstroke, a potentially fatal condition.

Insects thrive in warm environments. Insect repellant can keep away mosquitoes, black flies, and other insects. In tropical areas, repellant can also protect against bugs that carry diseases. Insect repellent may be purchased as a cream or spray and should be applied most during dusk, when insects are busiest.

HOW TO BUY GEAR

Depending on your sport of choice, you might need a lot of gear or very little at all. For example, in body boarding, the only equipment needed is a body board that costs roughly $100. However, other sports require drastically different equipment at differing costs. For example, for rock climbing, climbers have to purchase shoes, ropes, karabiners, pitons, a rock hammer, a chalk bag, and many other items; at the end of a shopping trip, these items may cost thousands of dollars.

In general, here is what to look for when buying gear:

- Before purchasing, try different pieces of equipment to see what fits best. Take advice from experienced athletes who can help you avoid mistakes in purchasing equipment.

- Be ready to pay for quality.

- Buy equipment that has been certified by a sport-governing body or national safety organization. For example, rock-climbing equipment should have a certification label from the Union Internationale des Associations d'Alpinisme (UIAA).

- Purchase only from reputable sources. If you do make the decision to buy secondhand equipment, have a professional take a look at it to check the quality or damage before buying.

Maintenance of equipment is also essential to safe action sports participation. This means more than just keeping things clean; you should also regularly check for damage, deterioration, and efficiency. Some

Equipment must be well maintained to remain effective. Climbing ropes and karabiners, for example, should be inspected for signs of wear and tear that might cause them to fail.

equipment may need to be examined by professionals every once in a while, but you should still check yourself for signs of wear and tear.

The right equipment is only helpful if it is maintained properly. A rope that might snap or a helmet snap that comes loose can be just as dangerous as not having the equipment at all. Learn maintenance techniques from books and experts, and always immediately address any concerns in equipment. For example, rope is extremely important in the well-being of a climber. Climbing rope is usually made from woven nylon, which is very strong and can withstand a lot of stress. However, it can still develop flaws, which may result in potentially lethal consequences. Here are some ways to maintain rope:

- Avoid walking over rope. When rope is caught between a foot and the rough ground, it can get scraped, and abrasions can wear out the fibers.

- Do not leave rope out in bright sunlight when not in use. UV rays can weaken it.

- Check the rope on a regular basis to look for cuts and fraying.

- Replace the rope after four years of very light use or after three months of very heavy use.

- Replace the rope immediately after a long fall, which may structurally weaken the rope.

- Wash a dirty rope with warm soapy water, and allow it to air dry. This helps clean the rope and expose any weaknesses or tears that were hidden when it was dirty.

Having the right equipment and following good maintenance practices will help give you piece of mind, so you can focus on performing. Mental preparation is vital, but physical preparation is equally important.

TEXT-DEPENDENT QUESTIONS:

1. Give some examples of a mental routine an extreme sports athlete might use to prepare for his or her activity.

2. For most action sports, what is the most important safety equipment?

3. What should an athlete look for when buying gear?

RESEARCH PROJECT:

Put together a maintanance checklist for the gear required for your favorite action sport. Describe the items that need to be examined and how often those checks should occur. Outline how you would repair or replace each item and what the risks are of improper maintenance of each item.

WORDS TO UNDERSTAND:

rupture: a break or tear in a part of the body

vascular system: also called the circulatory system; made up of the vessels that carry blood and lymph through the body—the arteries and veins carry blood throughout the body, delivering oxygen and nutrients to tissues and taking away waste matter

versatile: able to do many different things

Chapter 3

TRAIN FOR SUCCESS

Any sport likely would not be considered extreme if it did not take a toll on the body. Sprains, strains, dislocations, fractures, severe bruising, and lacerations are only a part of the long list of things that can happen to athletes. Fortunately, the chances of these injuries can be reduced through physical preparation. This preparation has three components—flexibility, strength, and endurance—all of which help protect against injuries.

WARM UP AND STRETCH

Muscles are not naturally flexible. It takes training to get them to be as flexible as an athlete needs. This means working to make them longer and give them a broader range of motion. Flexible muscles are also less likely to be damaged than tense muscles because they can endure more stress.

The importance of stretching the muscles ahead of time cannot be overstated. For each sport, a different set of muscles may need to be worked. For example, surfers and skiers should develop good flexibility in their legs to deal with twisting motions, especially in the hamstrings and quadriceps. Climbers need great flexibility in the hips and shoulders.

Never try to stretch when the body and muscles are cold. Cold muscles are inflexible and are more liable to **rupture** and be injured if subjected to sudden strain, so warming up should come first. A warm-up should consist of two elements: light exercise to raise the body temperature and stretching exercises to make muscle more flexible. Warm-up routines should be performed before any intense exercises or extreme sports. In outdoor conditions, they can be performed just about anywhere and take only about five minutes. However, in colder outdoor conditions, the warm-up period should be lengthened to ten to fifteen minutes to give the body longer to raise its temperature.

SIDEBAR

Extreme Wealth

Action sports athletes are rarely going to have the same earning potential as professional athletes in traditional, mainstream sports. Every so often, however, an extreme athlete comes along with the personality or entrepreneurial spirit to match his or her athletic talent. Here are ten of the most successful and their reported net worth:

1. TONY HAWK – skateboarding — $120M
2. BAM MARGERA – skateboarding — $45M
3. SHAUN WHITE – snowboarding — $20M
4. TRAVIS PASTRANA – freestyle motocross — $15M
5. ROB DYRDEK – skateboarding — $15M
6. RYAN SHECKLER – skateboarding — $10M
7. KELLY SLATER – surfing — $8M
8. LAIRD HAMILTON – surfing — $5M
9. PAUL RODRIGUEZ – skateboarding — $4M
10. DANNY KASS – snowboarding — $2.5M

Given all the twists and turns involved, surfers like superstar Kelly Slater (seen here surfing the Pipeline in Hawaii) need good flexibility in their legs.

Effective warm-up exercises include the following:

- Jog on the spot for about five minutes. Raise the knees higher and higher during the warm-up, although the thighs should not be above a forty-five-degree angle above the ground. Shake your arms and shoulders loosely to reduce upper body tension.

- Do the imaginary hula-hoop. Stand with your feet slightly apart and hands on your hips. Circle your hips in one direction as if you're spinning an imaginary hula-hoop and then in the opposite direction. Make large circles with your waist while maintaining your shoulders in as stable a position as possible.

- Do a windmill. To loosen the shoulders, circle your outstretched arms around while keeping them straight. Bring your hands together in front of you while they separate and brush the sides of your hips when they pass. Reverse direction after a few repetitions.

Climbing is tough on the ankles, so making sure they are stretched properly for maximum flexibility is an important training component.

Stretching routines and flexibility training differ from sport to sport. Various sets of stretching are specifically designed for a certain muscle group or range of motion.

ANKLES
(For Climbing, Skateboarding, Winter Sports, and Parachuting)

Sit comfortably on the ground. Place the left ankle over the right knee. Take hold of the left ankle with the left hand, and place the right hand over the toes and ball of the foot. Use the right hand to guide the foot in large circles, using the ankle as a pivot. Circle ten times in one direction and then change direction.

HIPS
(For Climbing, Surfing, Skiing, and Diving)

Standing with your feet shoulder width apart and hands on your hips, slowly bend yourself forward while moving your feet apart. Go down as close as you can to the ground while maintaining constant breathing. When you have reached your limit, maintain the position for about five to ten seconds. To come out of the position, move your feet slowly inward until you reach a standing position.

WAIST AND BACK
(For All Extreme Sports)

Standing with feet shoulder width apart, bend and reach straightforward from the waist, and lower your torso as far as possible, keeping the back straight. Hold the stretch for ten seconds, and then straighten yourself slowly. Then, with hands on the small of the back, stretch backward as far as possible. Hold the pose for ten seconds, and then straighten out your body.

SHOULDERS
(For Climbing, Mountain Biking, Skiing, Hang Gliding, and Parachuting)
Standing with feet shoulder width apart, hold your left arm straight out in front of you while linking the right arm around the left elbow. Keeping the left arm straight, use the right arm to pull until you feel the shoulder stretching. Hold this pose for ten seconds, and switch arms.

YOGA
Effective stretching is one of the benefits of yoga. Through yoga, a body can build muscle flexibility while releasing stiffness, tension, pain, and fatigue. It can increase the range of motion at the joints while also increasing flexibility in the ligaments, tendons, and fascia sheaths around the muscles. In the process of yoga, people also learn to breathe deeply and control their own bodies better. Furthermore, it promotes better balance.

Yoga can help athletes build strength, flexibility, and range of motion.

GET IN SHAPE

An important part of training for extreme sports involves working on conditioning the body. Conditioning tones the muscles and the cardiovascular system as well as builds strength in anticipation of the pressure placed on the body during strenuous activity.

There are different kinds of training that make up the components of

Planking is a good exercise for developing core muscles in the back and torso.

overall conditioning, including resistance training. Using only the body itself, resistance training strengthens muscle groups through basic movements such as sit-ups, crunches, push-ups, and squat thrusts. In contrast, weight training uses free weights and weight machines to develop muscles.

Free weights are **versatile** and relatively inexpensive, and they also simulate real-life lifting situations while promoting general body stabilization. However, machine weights can be just as effective in conditioning if weights are adjusted properly and a full range of motion is built into exercises. Weight training is generally a better tool for isolating a certain group of muscles than body-weight exercises, but it requires proper equipment and usage. The type of conditioning needed depends on the sport and the individual.

RESISTANCE TRAINING

External resistance can be used to cause muscles to contract. These repeated contractions increase muscle strength, tone, mass, and endurance. One of the common terms in resistance training is "carrying a load," where a load can refer to any weight, including the body itself. In these exercises, you brace your body by tensing certain muscles.

BACK

Developing strong core muscles can not only help reduce lower back pain but also make your body more resistant to injury. One exercise for your core muscles is the plank. Lie flat on your stomach while bracing the core muscles. Then raise your body up on your toes and elbows. Then, while the buttocks are flat and even to the shoulders, squeeze the navel toward the spine. Finally, hold this pose for thirty seconds, and eventually increase to two minutes as you become stronger.

KNEES

To protect your knees, it is crucial that the muscles surrounding and supporting the joint are strong. One exercise that works the quads is the straight leg raise. Lying flat on your stomach, brace your core muscles. Then, bend one leg up at the knee while keeping the other leg straight. Then tighten the quad muscles of the straightened leg, and slowly raise it parallel to the floor. Hold this position for five seconds, and then release both legs. Repeat ten times.

LEGS

Good balance starts with strong leg muscles. The wall shin raise is an exercise that will help accomplish this. Stand with your back and shoulders against the wall with your feet shoulder width apart about one foot (thirty centimeters) away from the wall. Then, raise your toes off the ground toward your body while maintaining your weight on the heels. Repeat ten times.

SHOULDERS

Shoulder exercises should result in a slight burning sensation but no more. One such exercise is the arm raise, usually practiced with a light weight or a band. Standing with your feet wide apart, slowly raise the arm holding the weight or band until it is shoulder level. Hold for about five seconds, and lower your arm. Repeat this process on each arm in two sets of ten. In this exercise, the back should not be used to lift, but instead, tension should be felt in the arm.

Weighted arm raises are effective in building shoulder strength.

> "When I finished my college ski racing career, I thought that I would never have to lift weights again and that my outdoor activities were enough to sustain my career as a professional. I've realized that lifting weight is about better functional and athletic movements, not bulking up.
>
> – Crystal Wright, two-time Freeskiing World Tour champion

WEIGHT TRAINING

Care and safety should be used when starting a weight training program. Here are some safety rules:

- Seek expert training from a professional in a proper gym, and do not persist if exercises become painful.

- Use a spotter who can stop any serious injuries or help in case of accidents.

- Employ correct techniques. When starting a new exercise, practice lifting the bare minimum to obtain correct motion before lifting with heavier weights.

- Instead of lifting extremely heavy weights, lift lighter weights with more repetitions.

- Add weights in increments of one to three pounds (half to one and a half kilograms). Do not add any more weight if you are struggling or are unable to maintain proper technique.

- Keep workout sessions to a maximum of three times a week at forty-five minutes per session to avoid overtraining. Muscles can be harmed if placed under too much stress and not given enough time to recuperate.

- Weight training is not about speed. It's important to breathe slowly at every stage of the exercise and to move slowly, spending some time stationary at each phase.

- Always remember to warm up.

Watch Canadian Olympic snowboarder Chris Robanske go through his off-season training routine.

PLYOMETRICS

Plyometric exercises work the muscle in two different ways. This means that a muscle is stretched (or loaded) before it is instantly contracted. An example of a plyometric exercise is a push-up with a clap in between. When the pectorals are elongated and loaded, they are then immediately contracted after the clap when the pectorals must push the body up again.

Athletes looking to improve their power, which is strength applied over a time period, train using plyometrics. In plyometrics, muscles not only have to contract at a certain strength, but they also have to contract quickly. Following are some examples of plyometric exercises.

RIM JUMP

This exercise uses body weight and gravity to load a muscle before the contraction to help increase the height of the vertical jump. While standing under a basketball rim, lower into a squat, keeping your back straight, and then jump as high as possible reaching for the rim. Alternate hands with each jump.

ANKLE HOPS

Athletes in most sports are always looking to increase their speed, which is typically done using sprint exercises. Another plyometric method for increasing speed is side-to-side ankle hops. In this exercise, a person has to hop about two to three feet (a half to full meter) from side to side while on one foot. The most stress is placed on the ankles and calves.

CARDIO TRAINING

To effectively train your cardiovascular system and boost endurance, training should increase your heart rate between 60 and 85 percent above its resting rate. While strengthening the lungs, heart, and **vascular system** of the body, cardio training can also help burn fat and extra calories. Experts recommend about twenty to sixty minutes of cardio per training session about three days a week. Low-intensity cardio, such as walking, requires longer durations (forty-five minutes to an hour), and the goal here is usually to burn fat while preserving joints. High-intensity cardio, such as Tae Bo, have shorter sessions (twenty to thirty minutes), and the goal is to burn calories and maintain a high metabolism.

Endurance training requires little equipment and almost zero expense. Some cardio exercises that burn the most calories include step aerobics, bicycling, swimming, running, rowing, and walking. High-intensity cardio exercises for those who are searching for high-intensity interval training (H.I.I.T.) include jumping rope, sprinting, and spinning.

Spinning is an example of a cardiovascular exercise.

TEXT-DEPENDENT QUESTIONS:

1. What are the three components to physical preparations?

2. Name some benefits of yoga.

3. What are some safety rules when starting a weight training program?

RESEARCH PROJECT:

Look into the sports that best complement your action sport and that occur in the season opposite to yours. Consider all aspects of what makes this sport a good complement, including similar use of the same movements and muscle groups, similar endurance or strength requirements, etc. Based on your research, indicate which sport you would pursue to complement your off-season training.

 ## WORDS TO UNDERSTAND:

impedes: interferes with or slows the progress of something

incoherent: not able to talk or express yourself in a clear way that can be easily understood

regimen: a plan or set of rules about food, exercise, etc., to make someone become or stay healthy

Chapter 4

TAKING CARE OF THE BODY: INJURIES AND NUTRITION

The spectrum of extreme sports is wide, as is the range of injuries that can occur while participating. For example, snowboarders injure their wrists, knees, and heads. When beginners are learning to snowboard, many stop by falling forward, and outstretched wrists can suffer sprains or fractures. Knees also suffer because they tend to absorb the shocks of snowboarding. Finally, crashes into objects or hard surfaces such as ice or snow can cause head trauma.

IMPACT INJURIES

More than 80 percent of injuries in snowboarding result from falls or collisions with other people and objects. This cause of injury is typical in extreme sports. Strain on limbs and the back during landings and collisions can also lead to injury, especially for parachutists. Some types of injuries include strains and sprains, where soft tissue

Eighty percent of snowboarding injuries result from falls or collisions.

such as muscles, tendons, and ligaments are damaged, and lacerations, which are cuts on the skin. Extreme sports accidents can also cause bone fractures and dislocations, especially in the arms, wrists, legs, shoulders, and ankles.

Falls on hard surfaces, like this skateboarding tumble, are a common cause of acute injuries like fractures and dislocations.

Bones that are fractured cause immediate pain, swelling, skin discoloration, and in severe cases, deformity (your body part will appear twisted or oddly shaped) and abnormal motion. Doctors are usually able to diagnose fractures based on X-rays. Most fracture injuries result from a significant force against bone, causing it to crack. Repetitive motions or forces against a certain bone can cause stress fractures.

A dislocation means that bones, which are usually connected at a joint, can be completely separated, usually disrupting blood flow and injuring nearby nerves and ligaments. Symptoms may include a bone visibly out of place, discolored skin, limited movement, swelling, and pain. Only a doctor can tell for sure if you have a dislocation. Dislocations usually result from a sudden impact to the joint.

SIDEBAR
Head and Neck Injuries

A 2014 study for the American Academy of Orthopaedic Surgeons (AAOS) found that in seven of the most popular action sports (surfing, mountain biking, motocross, skateboarding, snowboarding, snowmobiling, and snow skiing), nearly 4 million injuries were reported to have occurred between 2000 and 2011. Of these, 11.3 percent were of the head or neck variety, injuries that are very concerning due to their dangerous nature and the possibility of long-term effects. Here are some other findings of the study, as reported by the AAOS:

- The four sports with the highest incidence of head and neck injury (HNI) were skateboarding (129,600), snowboarding (97,527), skiing (83,313), and motocross (78,236).

- Concussions were the most common HNI among extreme sports participants. The risk of suffering a concussion was highest in snowboarding and skateboarding.

- Skateboarders also were found to have the highest risk of skull fractures.

- Surfers had the highest risk of neck fracture with a risk 38 times greater than skateboarders.

- The incidence of extreme sports HNIs increased from 34,065 in 2000 to 40,042 in 2010.

Fractures and dislocations are usually treated by realigning then immobilizing bones, done without surgery whenever possible. In cases where surgery is needed, bone fragments may be held in place while they heal with hardware such as surgical screws and/or metal plates. In both cases, a cast or splint is usually used to keep the healing area immobile. After removal, light weight training is advised initially to restore the range of motion, and weights should be added gradually in increments of one to three pounds (half to one and a half kilograms) until the place of injury has reached full range of movement and stability. Once the place of injury is fully healed, it should not feel painful during exercise.

*Snowboard legend
Shaun White spends a
day rehabbing an injury.*

OVERUSE INJURIES

Chronic injuries can occur in muscles, tendons, ligaments, bones, and joints and are caused by repetition of the same movements over a long period of time. Onset of symptoms is usually gradual and minor and could be easily ignored. Therefore, a medical professional should check any pain or physical annoyance that continues to persist. Some symptoms of overuse include the following:

- weakness, stiffness, pain, or limited movement in a joint or limb

- shooting or burning pains in a particular muscle group

- pains along with nausea or headaches

- a clicking or popping noise during a particular movement, accompanied with pain and a feeling of a loose joint

- a movement that feels inhibited or incomplete

- numbness in a joint

Overuse injuries are common in rock climbers, for example. Their fingers, hands, arms, and shoulders all undergo repetitive stress. Their muscles and tendons can be damaged by continuously being put under strain.

Overuse injuries are common in rock climbers. Their fingers, hands, arms, and shoulders all undergo repetitive stress.

Fingers are especially susceptible to ruptured tendons from holding too much weight during climbing. Over time, elbows tend to lose balance and have weakened joints because climbers can use their biceps more than the triceps or vice versa.

GETTING BETTER

No matter what the type of injury, athletes need to allow it to heal properly. With expert medical advice, athletes can properly heal and return to training. Many experts recommend a four-step process.

1. REST, ICE, COMPRESSION, ELEVATION (R.I.C.E.)

When an injury occurs, stop the activity, and immediately rest the injured limb or joint. Then, apply ice for no more than twenty minutes at a time, three or four times a day. Then wrap the injured area in clean compression bandages to avoid swelling and take anti-inflammatory medication. Finally, elevate the injured area. This process can take up to two weeks.

2. Range-of-Motion Exercises

Athletes should consult a doctor or physical therapist before beginning any range-of-motion exercises. These typically begin with simple exercises to test movement and progress to more complex movements. The goal of these exercises is to regain pain-free flexibility. The process can last three days to six weeks.

3. RESISTANCE EXERCISES

Once flexibility has returned, athletes should increase strength through resistance training. Begin with a rubber band as resistance, and slowly build up. Avoid any extreme heavy lifting. This phase should last one to six weeks.

4. RETURN TO TRAINING

Only after a doctor has determined that the injury has healed should the athlete start off with light training sessions and slowly increase the training **regimen** over a period of a few weeks until everything has returned to a pre-injury state. Allow one to six weeks for this stage.

Five months is the typical timeframe to complete all four phases. In cases where healing has been rushed or medical advice was not properly administered or followed, the area could be damaged again, possibly resulting in a disability that **impedes** further competition in any sport.

ENVIRONMENTAL INJURIES

Action sports pit athletes against the elements as well as each other, so extreme sports enthusiasts face the dangers of nature. These can lead to a variety of injuries.

MILD HYPOTHERMIA

Winter action sports like mountaineering, snowboarding, and skiing, along with many water-based action sports, are the ones where athletes face the threat of hypothermia. Normally, a healthy body temperature is about 98.6°F (36°C). In freezing air temperatures or during immersion in cold water, however, body temperature can fall below normal.

The first signs of mild hypothermia that become apparent are behavioral. A person will become tired and listless, with strange and sudden mood swings. He or she will have trouble concentrating and focusing on tasks, while his or her arms and legs will become uncoordinated and clumsy. He or she will look pale and his or her skin will be cold to the touch.

SEVERE HYPOTHERMIA

When the body temperature drops below 89.6°F (32°C), severe hypothermia takes hold, and the person's life is in danger. It has far more drastic symptoms. A person suffering from severe hypothermia tends to become **incoherent** and incapable of rational thought. Other symptoms include difficulty speaking, amnesia, and difficulty using his or her hands.

While waiting for medical treatment to arrive, try to keep the person warm by wrapping him or her in a warm blanket or sleeping bag. The goal is to gently warm up the body and heat areas where blood flow is close to the surface of the skin, such as wrists, armpits, back of the neck, small of the back, groin, and between the thighs.

Hypothermia is a real concern for athletes performing in cold water. Mild hypothermia can occur when the body's temperature drops below 98.6°F (36°C). When it drops below 89.6°F (32°C), severe hypothermia has set in, and the situation is deadly.

DEHYDRATION

In any climate, but particularly more so in hotter climates, dehydration is a very serious condition. Since most of the body is composed of water, when water input cannot meet the amount of water output, the body starts to malfunction.

People showing signs of dehydration should immediately be removed out of the open sunlight. Then, fluids need to be replaced slowly through drinking water, clear broths, or popsicles. In severe cases, where hospitalization is required, intravenous fluids can be administered if the patient is rejecting fluids orally.

NUTRITION

One of the most important aspects of becoming a healthier and better athlete is diet. Good nutrition can greatly benefit performance. The best way to get the nutrition you need is from healthy foods—but supplements can also help.

WHAT TO EAT

While a balanced diet is important for everyone, it is even more important for athletes. Typically, an athlete has to eat considerably more than a normal person. The United States Food and Drug Administration (FDA) suggests that the average American should eat about 2,000 calories a day; for a male high school- or college-level athlete, a diet averaging 3,000 to 4,000 calories is more common. For action sports athletes, the particular sport that they take part in will be an important factor in determining a nutritional plan as different extreme sports have different energy requirements. There are three main food groups to consider when choosing a diet: carbohydrates, protein, and fats.

> *I eat eggs a lot. This is a major source of protein for me. I usually eat a pile of greens, like arugula or baby kale, and then put a couple fried eggs on top with salsa or hot sauce.*
>
> — Jonathan Siegrist, who successfully completed four class 5.15 climbing routes

CARBOHYDRATES

Starchy foods contain carbohydrates, which is what the body breaks down to get energy. Starchy foods include breads, grains, and vegetables such as potatoes, cereal, pasta, and rice. There is no one-size-fits-all formula that can exactly dictate what an athlete's carb consumption should be. A general rule is that in

Carbohydrates in grain-based foods like bread, pasta, rice, and cereal provide athletes with a source of energy.

season or during times of intense training, athletes should eat about 5 grams (0.2 ounces) of carbs for every pound (0.5 kilogram) of body weight. In the off-season or during periods of lower training levels, it should be about 2 to 3 grams (0.07–0.10 ounces) per pound. The body uses carbs strictly for fuel, so if they are not being burned, they are turned into fat and stored. Therefore it is important to adjust carb intake based on activity level. Athletes should not eat heavily processed carbohydrates such as white sugar and white flour. These simple carbs are quickly broken down into sugars, which the body processes into fats if it does not immediately burn them off. The best carbohydrate choices for an athlete are complex types like pasta and whole-grain foods as well as starchy vegetables. A nutritious diet avoids empty calories or those provided by food that lacks other nourishment, like processed sugar and starches.

PROTEIN

Unlike carbohydrates, protein is used within the body. Proteins are important chemicals used to perform specific functions inside the body's cells. Our bodies can break down proteins that are found in foods and use them to build new proteins that make up our muscles and bones. During periods of intense training and activity, the body needs more protein to repair damage to muscles. Not eating enough protein can cause an athlete to lose muscle mass and negatively affect the ability to perform. The Academy of Nutrition and Dietetics recommends athletes consume about 0.50 to 0.75 gram (0.02–0.03 ounce) of protein for every pound (0.5 kilogram) of body weight. During the season or heavy training, that number should be closer to a full gram (0.04 ounces) per pound. This higher ratio is also true if an athlete is trying to build muscle mass. The best sources of proteins are lean meats and dairy products (such as milk or cheese) as well as eggs and certain types of soy, beans, and nuts.

FATS

Lots of times, we think of fats as bad for us because eating too much of them is unhealthy. However, fat is an important ingredient needed to make our bodies work correctly. They help balance hormone production, support cell growth, and protect our organs, among other functions. Without fats, our bodies cannot absorb certain vitamins as well as they should. Also, our skin and hair need some amount of fat to grow correctly. However, fats should still be eaten in moderation as they are higher in calories than protein or carbs. No more than 70 grams (2.5 ounces) a day is recommended. All fats are not created equal, however. Trans fats and saturated fats found in processed foods are high in bad cholesterol, which clogs arteries and is bad for the heart. The best sources of fat are vegetable oils, olive oil, and nuts.

DIETARY SUPPLEMENTS

Ideally, a balanced diet would provide the body with all the nutrients it needs. However, due to many varying factors, eating optimally is not always possible. Dietary supplements are available to fill dietary gaps created by a deficient diet.

In discussing dietary supplements here, this does not include banned performance-enhancing substances. Instead, the focus is on supplements that contain vitamins, minerals, and other compounds that help the body absorb nutrients or recover more efficiently. When properly used supplements can improve overall health and performance, but you should always consult a doctor or other expert before using them to augment your diet or training program. Some examples of common supplements include vitamin tablets and protein shakes or powder.

VITAMIN TABLETS

For many reasons, we do not always get the vitamins and nutrients we need. Often, this is because our diets are not as balanced as they should be. Sometimes, it is because the foods that are available to us have been processed in such a way that they lose nutrients. If you know or suspect that a certain key vitamin is underrepresented in what you are eating, in

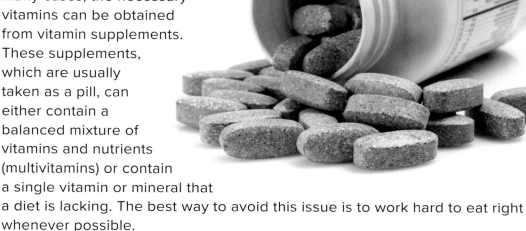

many cases, the necessary vitamins can be obtained from vitamin supplements. These supplements, which are usually taken as a pill, can either contain a balanced mixture of vitamins and nutrients (multivitamins) or contain a single vitamin or mineral that a diet is lacking. The best way to avoid this issue is to work hard to eat right whenever possible.

PROTEIN SUPPLEMENTS

Getting enough protein from the food you eat can be difficult as well. For athletes, eating protein immediately after a workout is recommended (to refuel the body), but most people either don't feel up to or do not have the time to spend cooking or preparing themselves a meal immediately after a workout or competition. That is where protein shakes come in handy. These are a protein supplement sold in powder form that look and taste like milkshakes when blended with water but contain no dairy products. Protein shakes deliver a high ratio of protein to carbohydrates and calories. They are not meant to replace meals. Many other necessary nutrients are gained from a balanced diet that cannot be replaced by protein shakes, regardless of how fortified they may be.

STAYING HYDRATED

The body needs water more than it needs any other nutrient. If you are not getting enough water, your performance will suffer in spite of any preparation or balanced diet. Dehydration occurs when your body doesn't have enough water. Symptoms include fatigue, dizziness, and headaches. No athlete can perform at his or her best if not properly hydrated. Proper hydration should be maintained not only in competition but throughout training as well. The body does not store water, so we need to constantly maintain its supply. The American College of Sports Medicine recommends these guidelines for athletes:

- Before Exercise: Drink 16 to 20 ounces (473–591 milliliters) within the two-hour period prior to exercise.

- During Exercise: Drink 4 to 8 ounces (118–237 milliliters) every fifteen to twenty minutes during exercise.

- Post Exercise: Replace 24 ounces (710 milliliters) for every pound (0.5 kilogram) of body weight lost during exercise

Whether you are a snowboarder, surfer, or speedboat racer, it is important to make sure you are hydrated. Extreme sports all have elements of danger that are amplified if the symptoms of dehydration occur.

Water is the body's most important nutrient. Athletes, like this mountain biker, need to carefully maintain their hydration levels.

TEXT-DEPENDENT QUESTIONS:

1. More than 80 percent of injuries in snowboarding result from what?

2. Name some sports where athletes face the threat of hypothermia.

3. How much water should an athlete consume before exercise?

RESEARCH PROJECT:

Put together a nutrition plan for an endurance athlete like a triathlete versus one for an anaerobic sport like snowboarding. Highlight and explain the key differences.

WORDS TO UNDERSTAND:

cohorts: friends or companions

pylons: a marking post or tower for guiding aviators, frequently used in races

stodgy: having very old-fashioned opinions or attitudes

Chapter 5

EXTREME SPORTS: FROM EMPTY POOLS TO THE EXTREME GAMES AND ESTONIA

COUNTERCULTURE AND THE X GAMES

Extreme sports, with a few exceptions, were developed in the 1970s and 1980s. Many extreme sport activities such as rock climbing and motorcycle racing have been around much longer, but they became specific action sport events during these decades. Motocross, for example, developed out of motorcycle racing, which has been around as long as the motorcycle itself. And although surfing was invented by Pacific islanders hundreds of years ago, the modern action sport of surfing came about within the last fifty years.

Rock climbing was around long before it became known as extreme.

The original extreme sports, however, were probably rock climbing and marathon running, both of which also grew beyond their beginnings in the 1970s. Other sports followed as a counterculture developed in the Western world with young people distancing themselves from what they saw as the safe, complacent lifestyle of their parents to forge a path of their own.

This path was considerably less safe as danger seemed to be the necessary element in the new sports of this generation. A perfect example was the new organization formed at Oxford University in England in 1979: the Dangerous Sports Club. These people intended to push the limits of their own safety. The club invented modern bungee jumping off of bridges around England. Next came BASE jumping (parachuting off of a bridge, antenna, span, or Earth formation, e.g., a cliff) then hang gliding in active volcanoes.

In America around the same time, three of the most well-known action sports came of age: BMX (bicycle motocross), snowboarding, and skateboarding. These were the new generations to take on bicycle racing and adaptation of surfing to land and snow. The next generation then added freestyle versions, taking these sports to the next level of danger.

Skateboarding took off in Southern California in the 1970s. Extremely dry weather caused a severe drought, and homeowners were forced to drain their swimming pools. To teenagers of the time who had been riding their skateboards on the street, the removal of the water revealed new canvases on which to create unique opportunities for danger. The momentum that allowed them to rise high above the lip of the pool was the catalyst for all sorts of new moves and tricks. These tricks evolved over the next twenty years, as did the places available to perform them, as skateboarders moved out of empty pools and parking lots to dedicated skate parks built exclusively for skateboarding. Companies sprang up around the sport making equipment and merchandise and sponsoring competitions and the top riders.

In the 1970s, while their warm-weather brethren were dropping into empty pools, cold-weather counterparts were figuring out how to surf on the snow. From

Skateboarding began gaining popularity with teenagers in Southern California in the 1970s.

steering with a rope attached to the tip of the board to using bindings to connect rider to board, snowboarding evolved along with its equipment. In the 1980s, skiing areas would not even allow snowboarders on the slopes. By the 1990s, however, snowboarding was so popular that **stodgy** ski resorts had to let the kids ride, and the sport was everywhere, formally sanctioned by the Fédération Internationale de Ski (FIS) or International Skiing Federation, the sport's international governing body, in 1994.

That was about the time skateboarding legend Tony Hawk noticed nine-year old Shaun White at a California skate park. Hawk is generally considered to be the best skateboarder ever and is certainly the most successful. He mentored White, who turned pro at age seventeen. White was also quite a prodigy on his snowboard, where he had paid sponsors at age seven. At seventeen, White made a name for himself at the Winter X Games, an extreme sports competition that was the cold-weather sport counterpart to the X Games, the warm-weather version started by sports network ESPN in 1995. White won two Winter X Games gold medals on his snowboard that year, 2003, and a legend was born. In the next two seasons, he won four more gold medals at the Winter X Games, setting up his Olympic debut in 2006 in Italy.

Although most of his success has come riding a snowboard, Shaun White is also an accomplished skateboarder and may compete in skateboarding events at the 2020 Olympics.

Snowboarding debuted as an Olympic sport in 1998 with two events for men and women. In 2006, White captivated the country by winning gold in his signature event, the halfpipe. In 2007, White won his first X Games gold medal on his skateboard with a victory in the vert event, which he won again in 2011. White would defend his Olympic gold medal in 2010 and win

BMX is one of the most popular action sports. It has evolved over the years from just racing to the more extreme freestyle events.

another seven Winter X Games gold medals to become the most famous snowboarder in the world. White has said he may compete in skateboarding in the 2020 Olympics, when the original counterculture action sport makes its Olympic debut in Tokyo.

Besides skate- and snowboarding, BMX was the other action sport of the 1970s to hit the mainstream. It started largely in the reservoir channels of Escondido, with teens riding their modified bikes from there into empty swimming pools and then following their skateboarding **cohorts** into skate parks. It took until 2008, but BMX racing is an Olympic medal sport as well.

DANGER AND ADRENALINE

Snowboarding, skateboarding, and BMX are certainly three of the most popular action sports in terms of participation, but the world of action sports has events that are much more extreme. BASE jumping, mentioned earlier, is one of the most dangerous activities there is. The BASE Fatality List, an unofficial database of BASE jumping deaths since 1981, went over 300 in 2016. More than 260 entries have occurred since the turn of the century. Fifteen jumpers were killed in August of 2016 alone. Many BASE jumping veterans blame wingsuits for the spike in fatalities. Wingsuits, which

BASE jumping is one of the most extreme of action sports and one of the world's most dangerous activities.

are basically specialized jumpsuits with extra fabric panels between the legs and under each arm, became commercially available in 1999 and prevalent in BASE jumping in 2003.

Also fraught with danger is "creeking." In this variation of canoeing or kayaking, athletes take on low-flow whitewater rapids. With low water volume, the rocks and other obstructions in the creek or river become more dangerous. Many experts say it is the most dangerous extreme sport in the world. The risks are twofold: smashing into jagged rocks is number one, but there is also a highly increased risk of getting trapped underwater if the canoe or kayak tips over. Obviously some sports are much more dangerous than others, but even more common action sports like snowboarding have their hazards. In February of 2017, four snowboarders were killed when they were buried in an avalanche near Tignes, France. All action sports have that adrenaline rush element of danger to them that makes them extreme.

Action sports are often classified by the element they are most commonly associated with: air, Earth, snow, or water. The annual Winter X Games are a celebration of many of the snow- and ice-based sports, including snowboarding, skiing, ice climbing, and snowmobiling. In the summer version, the X Games include many Earth sports like skateboarding, motocross, and BMX.

Although the X Games is the best-known showcase for action sports and a successful example of how these events can be organized, many action sports exist that are not included in the made-for-TV competition, especially in the air and water categories. Air racing involves pilots flying small aircraft

Ice climbing may no longer be included in the X Games, but there are still plenty of athletes out there scaling waterfalls in the winter.

through a series of huge **pylons** set up on the ground. Ice-climbing athletes armed with pick axes and crampons climb the faces of frozen waterfalls. On the ocean, two-person teams race forty-foot (twelve-meter) powerboats at speeds of more than one hundred fifty miles per hour (two hundred forty kilometers per hour). Extreme skyrunning involves footraces at altitudes above a mile (two thousand meters) at a 30 percent incline over rough terrain with no trails.

SIDEBAR

Free Soloing

Free soloing is one of the most dangerous of all extreme sports. It is the term given to climbing rock faces without any safety equipment—no ropes or support of any kind. Only the climbers' hands, feet, and strength keep them from falling. The only assistance comes from a chalk bag strapped around the waist, which is used to keep the hands dry. To many climbers, this is the essence of climbing, relying only on climbing skill and the personal patience and will to make the ascent. Why is this enough, though, to risk certain death if a mistake is made?

Take the world's most famous living free soloist, American Alex Honnold. Honnold has climbed several of the world's most difficult faces with his bare hands, yet he spends the majority of his time climbing more conventionally, with rope and a partner. He says he does the free solo climbs "because it's so much fun." Honnold rejects the idea that he is an adrenaline junkie, saying, "If I get a rush, it means that something has gone horribly wrong because the whole thing should be pretty slow and controlled."

Lack of control is why Honnold considers BASE jumping to be too dangerous, an interesting position for someone who seems oblivious to the possibility of his own death when he is clinging to a sheer rock face by the tips of his fingers and shoes. As for the other, far less-accomplished climbers who continue to risk death with every send they attempt, it is seen as an absolute freedom, a deep meditation with total self-awareness and clarity of mind. The satisfaction derived from this somehow outweighs the real possibilities of the worst outcome.

The question of what it is that attracts athletes to these extreme, dangerous pursuits has often been asked. What is it that makes a person say, "I need to jump out of this perfectly good airplane?" Obviously that is an inherently dangerous thing to do. Well, as it turns out, that is exactly the point. Scientists have produced evidence that danger is a lure for extreme athletes. The culprit is a chemical called dopamine, which is produced in the brain and induces feelings of happiness after a dangerous situation has been successfully navigated. It is a true chemical high, and it can be habit forming in some people. They seek situations that cause them fear, so they can feel that rush of satisfaction when the fear passes.

For other people the high is psychological rather than chemical. Setting and then achieving very challenging physical goals gives them a deep sense of satisfaction. It is not about the competition but rather the accomplishment. Training goals that are met can be just as satisfying as winning events as long as the goal is extreme enough for the individual. Dopamine and adrenaline have their roles, but the psychological thrill can produce the biggest rush in some extreme athletes.

THE MAINSTREAM AND THE FUTURE

Extreme sports have become a multibillion-dollar enterprise, driven by the inclusion of many events in the high-profile X Games, and even more so with the addition of several events to the Olympic Games in subsequent years. With exposure has come acceptance, and these fringe sports practiced by long-haired, tattooed slackers are now seen as legitimate competitions with real athletes. The 2014 Winter Olympic Games in Sochi, Russia, saw nine new action sport events added to the roster. In

The rush of satisfaction when succeeding at a dangerous trick is one of the effects of the brain chemical dopamine.

2018 in Peyongchang, the big air event will make its Olympic debut in the snowboarding category.

Mainstream recognition is certainly not limited to the winter edition. The 2020 Summer Olympics in Tokyo are also set to expand in an extreme way. New additions will include men and women's shortboard surfing, street and park versions of skateboarding, and two sport climbing events (bouldering and lead). Shortboards are used by pro surfers to give them more speed and better maneuverability but are less stable than traditional longboards. Street skateboarding uses obstacles like stairs, handrails, and park benches as part of the course. Park skateboarding refers to skate park features like halfpipes and other incline features. Bouldering involves climbing with no ropes up a short course (usually less than twenty feet [six meters]) by figuring out the best path to the top from a given start position. In lead climbing, a two-person team works to climb a course with a rope used to prevent falls. The International Olympic Committee has recognized that to keep younger audiences interested and make them ongoing Olympics fans, they need to keep the games fresh and modern, including the sports that appeal to the new generation of athletes and fans.

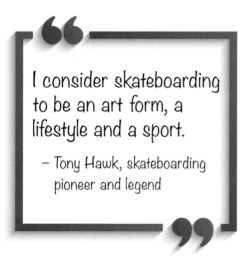

I consider skateboarding to be an art form, a lifestyle and a sport.

– Tony Hawk, skateboarding pioneer and legend

The X Games, meanwhile, continue to lead the way in making the extreme mainstream. Purists will say that these sports are losing the counterculture aspect that attracted the orginal stars like Tony Hawk, Dave Mirra, and Travis Pastrana to them in the first place. The X Games, however, are even bigger than ever two decades beyond their debut.

Summer X Games 2016 was held in Austin, Texas, with skateboarding, BMX, and motorcycle events. Based on the results there, the future looks bright for Brazil's Pâmela Rosa. At just sixteen years old, Rosa won X Games gold in the skateboard street event at both X Games Oslo (the European installment of the games) and X Games Austin. This made Rosa the youngest woman ever to win the event.

Winter X Games XXI, held in January 2017 at Aspen, Colorado, featured twenty events in skiing, snowboarding, and snowmobiling. These games featured young stars of the future Kelly Sildaru and Marcus Kleveland.

Sildaru, a freestyle skier from Estonia, took the gold medal in the skiing slopestyle event, defending her title from 2015. At just fourteen years old, Sildaru is the youngest person, male or female, to win two X Games gold medals. Like many extreme athletes, Sildaru made a name for herself in the freestyle community on YouTube well before international event medals came into play.

Watch teen phenom Kelly Sildaru showing her skills at age eight in *Wanted*.

Marcus Kleveland is a snowboarder from Norway. He was *Snowboarder Magazine's* Rookie of the Year for 2016 at age seventeen. He is known for having great body awareness and board control. The following year at Winter X Games XXI, Kleveland won gold in the snowboard slopestyle competition. The win was unexpected as the X Games field was stacked with much more experienced and accomplished riders, like six-time gold medalist Mark McMorris of Canada.

Kleveland also won silver in the big air event at those 2017 Winter X Games and actually got more notoriety for this than for the event that he won. This

Snowmobiling is one of the three event categories at the Winter X Games.

is because during the big air event, he became the first person to ever land a Quad Cork in compeition, one of the most difficult tricks there is. As his peers would undoubtedly say, Kleveland stomped an amazing run.

Not all extreme sports phenoms compete in X Games-eligible events. Most extreme sports are not represented at the X Games. Many, like climbing or inline skating, for example, have been tried at the X Games and lasted anywhere from one year to several. Ultimately, however, ESPN decided that events that do not demonstrate progression, hold or grow in popularity, or lack a commercially viable surrounding industry are discontinued.

Therefore New Yorker Ashima Shiraishi may never compete at the X Games. The rock-climbing phenom collects her accolades elsewhere. In 2016 at just fifteen years old, Shiraishi became the first woman to ever scale, or "send"

Inline skating, one of the original X Games events in 1995, was dropped from the program in 2005.

in climbing terms, a V15 graded boulder problem when she conquered Horizon at Hiei in Japan. She also repeated as the International Federation of Sports Climbing World Youth champion in both the bouldering and lead events.

Action sports athletes continue to progress, and records continue to fall, the measure of a true sport for some experts, rather than simply doing the same things with the same results merely for the thrill of it. That does not mean kids are not still dreaming up new and inventive extreme activities. Who knows what the modern equivalent to the empty swimming pool will be? Twenty years from now, however, some teenager might win an Olympic medal for mastering it.

TEXT-DEPENDENT QUESTIONS:

1. Skateboarding took off in Southern California in the 1970s due to an environmental situation across the region. What happened?

2. Name three of the most dangerous activities extreme sports athletes participate in.

3. Name a few of the new extreme summer sports slated to come to the 2020 Summer Olympics in Tokyo.

RESEARCH PROJECT:

Look up and write short descriptions of the relatively new action sports of river bugging, skishing, and powerski jetboarding. Add two more action sports to your report that are not mentioned in this book that are relatively new.

SERIES GLOSSARY OF KEY TERMS

Acute Injury: usually the result of a specific impact or traumatic event that occurs in one specific area of the body, such as a muscle, bone, or joint.

Calories: units of heat used to indicate the amount of energy that foods will produce in the human body.

Carbohydrates: substances found in certain foods (such as bread, rice, and potatoes) that provide the body with heat and energy and are made of carbon, hydrogen, and oxygen.

Cardiovascular: of or relating to the heart and blood vessels.

Concussion: a stunning, damaging, or shattering effect from a hard blow—especially a jarring injury of the brain resulting in a disturbance of cerebral function.

Confidence: faith in oneself and one's abilities without any suggestion of conceit or arrogance.

Cooldown: easy exercise, done after more intense activity, to allow the body to gradually transition to a resting or near-resting state.

Dietary Supplements: products taken orally that contain one or more ingredient (such as vitamins or amino acids) that are intended to supplement one's diet and are not considered food.

Dynamic: having active strength of body or mind.

Electrolytes: substances (such as sodium or calcium) that are ions in the body regulating the flow of nutrients into and waste products out of cells.

Flexible: applies to something that can be readily bent, twisted, or folded without any sign of injury.

Hamstrings: any of three muscles at the back of the thigh that function to flex and rotate the leg and extend the thigh.

Hydration: to supply with ample fluid or moisture.

Imagery: mental images, the products of imagination.

Mind-Set: a mental attitude or inclination.

Overuse Injury: an injury that is most likely to occur to the ankles, knees, hands, and wrists, due to the excessive use of these body parts during exercise and athletics.

Plyometrics: also known as "jump training" or "plyos," exercises in which muscles exert maximum force in short intervals of time, with the goal of increasing power (speed and strength).

Positive Mental Attitude (PMA): the philosophy that having an optimistic disposition in every situation in one's life attracts positive changes and increases achievement.

Protein: a nutrient found in food (as in meat, milk, eggs, and beans) that is made up of many amino acids joined together, is a necessary part of the diet, and is essential for normal cell structure and function.

Quadriceps: the greater extensor muscle of the front of the thigh that is divided into four parts.

Recovery: the act or process of becoming healthy after an illness or injury.

Resistance: relating to exercise, involving pushing against a source of resistance (such as a weight) to increase strength. Strength training, or resistance exercises, are those that build muscle. They create stronger and larger muscles by producing more and tougher muscle fibers to cope with the increasing weight demands.

Strategy: a careful plan or method.

Stretching: to extend one's body or limbs from a cramped, stooping, or relaxed position.

Tactics: actions or methods that are planned and used to achieve a particular goal.

Tendon: a tough piece of tissue in the body that connects a muscle to a bone.

Training: the process by which an athlete prepares for competition by exercising, practicing, and so on.

Warm-Up: exercise or practice especially before a game or contest—broadly, to get ready.

Workout: a practice or exercise to test or improve one's fitness for athletic competition, ability, or performance.

FURTHER READING:

Hurley, Michael. *Board Sports (Extreme Sports)*. Raintree, 2015.

Killcoyne, Hope Lourie. *Extreme Sports and Their Greatest Competitors (Inside Sports)*. Rosen Education Service, 2015.

Luke, Andrew. *Extreme Sports (Inside the World of Sports)*. Broomall, PA: Mason Crest, 2017.

INTERNET RESOURCES:

The American Sports Medicine Institute: *http://www.asmi.org/*

ESPN X GAMES: *http://xgames.espn.go.com/xgames/*

FDA: Dietary Supplements:
http://www.fda.gov/Food/DietarySupplements/default.htm

Web MD:
http://www.webmd.com/fitness-exercise/extreme-sports-whats-appeal

VIDEO CREDITS:

Watch Danny Way get ready to jump the Great Wall of China on his skateboard. *http://x-qr.net/1GqY*

Mountaineer and BASE jumper Joby Ogwyn talks about the mental toughness needed to climb Mount Everest. *http://x-qr.net/1Fvv*

Watch Canadian Olympic snowboarder Chris Robanske go through his off-season training routine. *http://x-qr.net/1HFJ*

Snowboard legend Shaun White spends a day rehabbing an injury. *http://x-qr.net/1DTu*

Watch teen phenom Kelly Sildaru showing her skills at age eight in *Wanted*. *http://x-qr.net/1Dji*

PICTURE CREDITS

QR CODES AND LINKS TO THIRD-PARTY CONTENT

INDEX

In this index, page numbers in ***bold italics*** font indicate photos or videos.

ABOUT THE AUTHOR

Peter Douglas is a former journalist, reporting on both sports and general news for many years at television stations in various locations across the US affiliated with NBC, CBS and Fox. Prior to his journalism career he worked with the Boston Red Sox Major League baseball team. An avid writer and sports enthusiast, he has authored 16 additional books on sports topics. In his downtime Peter enjoys family time with his wife and two young children and attending hockey and baseball games in his home city.